ARE YOU SKILLED IN THE WORD OF RIGHTEOUSNESS?

D1568937

By Dwayne Norman

Empyrion Publishing
Winter Garden FL

Are You Skilled in the Word of Righteousness?
ISBN: 978-0692263006
Copyright © 2014 by Dwayne Norman

Empyrion Publishing
Winter Garden FL
info@EmpyrionPublishing.com

Unless otherwise indicated, all Scripture quotations are taken
from the New King James Version of the Bible.

CHAPTER
1

THE WORD
OF
RIGHTEOUSNESS

One of the greatest revelations of our redemption is, knowing we are the righteousness of God in Christ. I'm talking about every Christian. We are as righteous as God! Think about that. The Bible doesn't say we have a certain degree of the righteousness of God. It says we have been made as righteous as God is (II Corinthians 5:21)! That is an enormous statement, but our God said it and we need to believe it! Whether our head understands it or not, it's still true. Don't let your past life and all the times you have missed it cloud your believing. God didn't tell us we are as righteous as He is because of our personal works. Listen, the only reason we are as righteous as God, is because we are in Christ! If we were not washed white as snow through Jesus' Blood, then our righteousness would be as filthy rags. Remember, as Christians, we are not alone. What I mean is we are in Christ. Our lives are no longer about who we are without Jesus. It's about who we are in Him. Just think, if we were totally immersed in the reality of this truth, the devil would never succeed in condemning us again. I didn't say he wouldn't try to condemn us. I said he would not succeed, because we would not listen to him. We would ignore the thoughts the devil speaks into our minds, because our Heavenly Father's voice speaking in our hearts is much louder. We would hear our Father God constantly reminding us, "You are My righteousness in Christ".

When you read the four Gospels you see that the devil could never touch Jesus, no matter how much he tried, because Jesus knew how to walk in righteousness. The devil couldn't do anything to Jesus until He allowed him to, when He suffered for us and went to the cross. In John 14:30, Jesus said, **"...the ruler of this world is coming, and he has nothing in Me."** He was saying the devil can't touch me. He has no place in my life. You see, the devil can't get a hold

4

of righteousness. Righteousness repels the devil and everything he stands for. The devil cannot hang onto righteousness. I think it would be like grabbing hold of a burning hot coal. You would release that quickly. Now the devil can get a hold of sin. He can grip that and use it to gain a stronghold in a person's life, but he has to back off from righteousness. He does not want us to understand and walk in the reality of our righteousness in Christ. Daily living in this kind of reality will prevent the devil from gaining any footholds in our lives.

Remember when the Lord preached His first sermon in Nazareth (Luke 4)? Instead of receiving His message they were filled with wrath and took Him up to the top of a hill on which the city was built to throw Him off. Luke 4:30 says, **"Then passing through the midst of them, He went His way."** He just passed through the midst of them, and they couldn't touch or hold onto Him. God didn't give Him a machine gun to shoot them, and He didn't send an angel down to smite them. He just passed through them unharmed. It didn't say they quickly dispersed so Jesus could get through. The devil wanted to get a hold of Jesus through the people and throw Him off the cliff, but he couldn't touch Him.

God wants His children to be so skilled in the word of righteousness, in the reality that they are God's righteousness, that they can pass right through sickness, disease, poverty, sin and all the works of the devil. Nothing from the kingdom of darkness can touch us! It's repelled away from us as we go through each day! We should be so developed in this revelation that our enemy has no place in us. He can't find anywhere to get a foothold; therefore he can't develop any strongholds in our lives!

This book is by no means an exhaustive study of this subject, but it's enough to help Christians move in the right direction in gaining a greater reality of their righteousness in Christ. The Lord inspired me to write this book after reading Hebrews 5:11-14.

"Of whom we have much to say, and hard to explain, since you have become <u>dull of hearing</u>.

For though by this time you ought to be teachers, you need someone to teach you again the first principles of the oracles of God; and you have come to need milk and not solid food.

For <u>everyone who partakes only of milk is unskilled in the word of righteousness</u>, for he is a babe.

But solid food belongs to those who are of full age, that is, those who by reason of use have their senses exercised to discern both good and evil."

The writer of this letter said these Believers should already be teachers. They should be past having to be taught the first or basic principles of God. Spiritually speaking, he said they were not eating solid food yet, and they should have been. They were only partaking of milk, which meant they were still babies. In I Peter 2:2, the Apostle Peter said, **"As newborn babes, desire the pure milk of the word, that you may grow thereby."** Yes, milk is good and we grow by drinking milk, but at some point we need to start eating solid food. Hebrews Chapter 5 said if all you partake of is milk, you're a babe, and unskilled in the Word of righteousness. Therefore, to be a mature Christian, you must be skilled in the <u>Word of</u> <u>righteousness</u>. II Timothy 3:16 tells us how to get skilled.

"All Scripture is given by inspiration of God, and is profitable for doctrine, for reproof, for correction, for <u>instruction in righteousness</u>."

It's through the Scriptures that we are taught and instructed in the Word of righteousness. Another point that he brought out in Hebrews 5:11 is, they were dull of hearing. I believe this is a reason why they weren't teachers skilled in the Word of righteousness. In the Greek, in which this was written, the word "dull" means slow and sluggish. They were slow to hear, in comparison to quick to hear. I've always felt that the phrase to be quick to hear means to be quick to learn, and to apply every effort to gain knowledge and understanding. It sounds like these Believers weren't really trying to grow up spiritually. They were satisfied just to drink milk and remain at their current spiritual level. Listen to this prophecy the Lord Jesus quoted from Isaiah.

"And in them the prophecy of Isaiah is fulfilled, which says: 'Hearing you will hear and shall not understand, and seeing you will see and not perceive;
For the hearts of this people have grown <u>dull</u>. Their ears are hard of hearing, and their eyes they have closed, lest they should see with their eyes and hear with their ears, lest they should understand with their hearts and turn, so that I should heal them."
Matthew 13:14, 15

So if we become dull of hearing, then we will not understand with our hearts and we will not be healed. He's not just referring to healing for our bodies, but to whatever we need from the Lord. Therefore, let's be quick to hear and quick to be conformed to the image and stature of Christ! I want you to see Hebrews 5:11-14 out of the Amplified Bible.

"Concerning this we have much to say which is hard to explain, since you have become dull in your [spiritual] hearing and sluggish [even slothful in achieving spiritual insight].

For even though by this time you ought to be teaching others, you actually need someone to teach you over again the very first principles of God's Word. You have come to need milk, not solid food.

For everyone who continues to feed on milk is obviously inexperienced and unskilled in the doctrine of righteousness (of conformity to the divine will in purpose, thought, and action), for he is a mere infant [not able to talk yet]!

But solid food is for full-grown men, for those whose senses and mental faculties are trained by practice to discriminate and distinguish between what is morally good and noble and what is evil and contrary either to divine or human law."

When the Lord said solid food belongs to those who are of full age (mature), the question might be asked, what is solid food? If we know what God considers "solid food" and we spend time eating it, we won't be babies anymore. Well, according to these verses, solid food is the Word of righteousness. When you are skilled or developed in that Word, then it's a good sign you're a mature Christian; or as the Bible says you are of full age. In the next three verses, Hebrews 6:1-3, the Spirit of God reminds them of six basic principles that all Christians should be established in.

"Therefore, leaving the discussion of the <u>elementary</u> principles of Christ, let us go on to perfection, not laying again the foundation of repentance from dead works and of faith toward God,
Of the doctrine of baptisms, of laying on of hands, of resurrection of the dead, and of eternal judgment.
And this we will do if God permits."

The writer said these are basic or elementary principles they needed to be established in before he could give them solid food to eat. These six principles were very important, but they represented the milk of the Word, and not solid food. They were the first principles. This implies if you're only established in these principles, then you're still a baby Christian. He spoke to them as if he wasn't sure if God would allow him to feed them solid food. It sounds to me like they still had not partaken of enough milk to move on to solid food. So, these six principles are vital to our spiritual growth, but once fully grounded in them, we need to move on to solid food. We must get skilled in the Word of righteousness!

He said we must go on to perfection or maturity, not laying again these six principles. When he said "not laying again", he wasn't saying these teachings weren't important. He was saying there is more we need to learn and understand. We need to go on to everything else the Lord has for us. We don't have room in this book to teach on these six principles, but study them out yourself, and get grounded in them. If you're not established in these truths, I would recommend that you do that first, and then the Word of righteousness will be a greater reality to you.

I think some Christians struggle to learn and understand God's Word because they're trying to digest solid food before partaking of the milk of God's Word. They're having a hard time spiritually swallowing some truths from God's Word because they're not ready for it. They need to finish drinking their milk.

If you noticed in the Amplified Bible it referred to the doctrine of righteousness, instead of the Word of righteousness. There are many doctrines of the Lord and this is a very important one. For further understanding of the importance of doctrine, see our book "Defending the Faith". Doctrine is teaching, or the teachings of God's Word. When we talk about the word righteousness, there are two points I want to bring out. Number 1, righteousness can be used in a general sense to mean doing what is right in God's eyes, or conforming to His Divine will and purpose. In Matthew Chapter 3, the Lord Jesus asked John to baptize Him. John tried to prevent Him. He said I must be baptized by you. I don't blame John. I would have said the same thing. The Lord responded by saying He must fulfill all righteousness. We know Jesus was sinless and morally perfect; so He wasn't saying that He needed to be made righteous. He was using the word in a general sense to say I must fulfill God's will for my life. He was saying I'm here to conform to God's Divine plan (John 6:38).

Number 2, righteousness is used in a very specific way to refer to the kind of nature we have as new creations in Christ. It's this second meaning I want us to look at right now. Being skilled or developed in this area of righteousness will better equip us to yield and submit ourselves to God for the fulfillment and conformity of His Divine will and purpose in our lives. The Apostle Paul said, **"Awake to righteousness, and do not sin..."** (I Corinthians 15:34) In W.E. Vine's dictionary on Greek New Testament words, the word "awake" **suggest a return to soberness of mind from the stupor consequent upon the influence of evil doctrine.** Remember, the Bible said they were dull (sluggish) of hearing. Many Christians are dull of hearing or they're in a mental stupor because they've been listening to evil doctrines. An evil doctrine means wrong teachings: doctrines of demons and doctrines of men. If we listen to teaching contrary to God's Word, we're being influenced by evil doctrines.

We need to return to soberness of mind. Our minds need to be renewed to the Word of God, and in this case, to the Word of righteousness. We can miss out on a lot of wonderful things from the Lord when we're spiritually asleep. We need to wake up and pay attention to what God is saying and doing! Let me remind you of what happened to the disciples on the Mount of Transfiguration. Jesus took Peter, James and John up on a mountain to pray. The appearance of His face was altered, and His robe became white and glistening, and Moses and Elijah appeared in glory and began to speak to Him; but His disciples were asleep when this began. Verse 32, in Luke 9 says,

"But Peter and those with him were heavy with sleep; and <u>when</u> <u>they were fully awake, they saw</u> His glory and the two men who stood with Him."

Please notice, they didn't see anything until they awoke. Many Christians are spiritually, heavy with sleep (a stupor-dull of hearing). They are the very ones who say, "I don't ever see God do anything. I don't ever hear His voice. I never get Divine direction from the Lord." It's hard to see anything when you're asleep and your eyes are closed. Let's wake up! Let's open up our spiritual eyes, ears and hearts to the revelation and understanding of righteousness; that is, who we are in Christ and who He is in us! In the King James Bible, I Corinthians 1:30 says,

"But of him are ye in Christ Jesus, who of God is made unto us wisdom, and righteousness, and sanctification, and redemption."

Jesus is God's righteousness in us. It's not about our righteousness apart from Him, because we have none. It's about who He is in us and who the Father has made us in Him!

Look at II Corinthians 5:21 in the King James Bible.
"For he hath made him to be sin for us, who knew no sin; that we might be <u>made</u> the righteousness of God in him."

Romans 5:19 says:
"For as by one man's disobedience many were made sinners, so also by one Man's obedience many will be <u>made</u> righteous."

I underlined the word made in those verses to draw your attention to it. Remember, Jesus never committed any sin when He walked on earth or went to the cross. God made Him to be sin for us. If it wasn't for you and me, God would have never made Jesus to be sin. The Father didn't go and find some sin just anywhere that He could use to put on Jesus. He took our sins and our entire sin nature (the law of sin and death) and laid it on Jesus when He went to the cross (Isaiah 53:6). God could not make us righteous until our penalty for sin was paid and removed out of our lives. Romans 4:25 says,

"Who was delivered up because of our offenses, and was raised because of our justification."

If you look closely at that verse, it tells you why Jesus was raised from the dead. He was raised because of our justification. Another way to say that is, God did not raise Jesus from the dead until He could declare us justified. To be justified means to be declared righteous. You might ask the question, "Why did God wait 3 days and nights before raising Jesus up?" I don't know, but I guarantee you, as a father, God didn't want His Son to suffer one second more than was necessary. But the Lord Jesus had to suffer and pay our penalty for sin until the laws of justice were satisfied and God could legally make us righteous.

We've been <u>made</u> righteous. Some Christians think they are still sinners, and to be made righteous simply means they are cleaner sinners than they used to be. If you are born again, you are not a sinner anymore. You can still commit sins if you so choose, but you are not a sinner (meaning one who is spiritually dead). Remember, to be spiritual dead doesn't mean your spirit can't be reborn, and it doesn't mean you cease to exist. It means that spiritually you are separated from God and from His life. You would be living in the kingdom of darkness instead of the Kingdom of God. We were made sinners through Adam's sin, but we have been made righteous through Jesus' obedience. We are not sinners saved by grace! We were sinners who got saved by grace, and now we are God's righteousness in Christ! We need to realize that we are operating in a greater righteousness than the Old Testament saints. In the Old Covenant, righteousness could only be <u>accounted</u> to God's people. They could not be <u>made</u> righteous. Having God's righteousness accounted to you is different than being made His righteousness.

Romans 4:3 declares:

"For what does the Scripture say? "Abraham believed God, and it was accounted to him for righteousness.""

The word accounted means imputed, reckoned, credited or counted. Because of Abraham's faith, God counted him righteous, even though he wasn't. You could say God gave him a credit to his personal account. As a result of his faith in what Jesus <u>was going to do</u> at Calvary, God allowed him to live in right standing with Him. He couldn't make him righteous. God couldn't give Abraham a new nature or cleanse his conscious before Calvary (Read Hebrews 9:9,14; 10:1,2), but He could allow him to operate in a right standing. It wasn't because of Abraham's good works, because he still had the nature of sin and death in his spirit all his life. No one could actually be changed on the inside and receive a new nature or conscience until Jesus died and arose from the dead. He wasn't in right standing because he obeyed the law, for it didn't come until Moses was born. It was solely because of his faith in God; so that it might be freely by God's grace. In other words, a <u>gift</u>!

Romans 5:17 says:

For if by the one man's (Adam) offense death reigned through the one, much more those who receive <u>abundance of grace</u> and of the <u>gift of righteousness</u> will reign in life through the One, Jesus Christ."

Please grab a hold of this understanding. When you and I received Jesus as our personal Lord and Savior, we were given abundance of grace and the gift of righteousness. The lifestyle you were living, whether good or bad, was irrelevant when you met Jesus. No matter how much you thought you didn't deserve His righteousness, was irrelevant when you came to Lord. His righteousness was a gift that He gave you. You don't pay for a gift; that's why it's a gift. If someone says to me, "I want to give you a gift and it will cost you $10.00", then it's not a gift. If it's a gift to me, it will be free of charge. For hundreds of years the Church has struggled in accepting God's gift of righteousness, as a gift. Man's religion has brainwashed many in the Church to believe that righteousness is solely based on your works; which would be a result of man's efforts, not faith in God.

I think some Christians have the idea that if they demonstrate enough good works in their outward life, then at some point, almost miraculously, they will be changed on the inside. Listen! It's just the opposite of that! Good works or outward holiness should be the fruit produced from inward righteousness. The greater revelation I have of my righteousness in Christ, the holier my life should be, so if you take a Christian that is living in and out of sin, it's a sure sign he's not skilled in the Word of righteousness. That's why it is so important we meditate and study these Scriptures, and get grounded in them; so God can drastically change our lives! The power in His Word will greatly affect the way we talk, live and act!

Please understand, when you and I were born-again, we were born over again; not physically but spiritually. When we were born-again, we were born righteous. That's when God gave us this wonderful gift. The way to experience a gift from someone is simply to accept it. You don't have to struggle or work up anything; or show them a resume of all the good things you've done. You just reach out and take it. Whether you realize it or not, that's what you did when you got saved. By faith, you reached out and took God's gift. If you are struggling to use your gift, then you haven't accepted it as free. I heard one minister tell the story of a Christian man who came to him struggling concerning righteousness. To help him better understand, the minister asked, "Sir, are you a man or woman?" Surprised, the man said, "Well, I'm a man." The minister said, "How did you become a man?" He said, "I was born that way." The minister responded, "Well, that's how you became righteous. You were born that way." You and I don't have to spend our lives trying to become righteous, we were born that way. God made us righteous when we were born-again.

We didn't have to develop our faith for six months in hope that it would be strong enough to receive the gift of righteousness. This was not something we had to spiritually struggle with to receive. It was so simple and easy. As soon as we said yes to Jesus, and accepted Him as our Lord and Savior, we were instantly <u>made</u> righteous! God did it for us! We didn't do it. From now on, we should spend our lives walking in our righteousness in Christ, and demonstrating it in our daily lives!

If that didn't register with you, let me say it a different way. When God gave us His righteousness as a gift, and called it a gift, that was His way of identifying to us that it was free. But based on II Corinthians 5:21, that says He <u>made</u> us righteous in Christ; His gift of righteousness was actually more than a gift. His generosity went beyond our understanding of a gift. He did far more than we've conceived. Here's what I mean. If I gave you the gift of a car, it would be freely yours to do with as you please. Even though the car belongs to you, it doesn't <u>make</u> you a car. I gave you a wonderful gift, but you didn't become the gift. You and the car are two separate entities. God didn't give us the gift of righteousness as if it's something we can carry around in our brief case. The Lord did what man can't do when he bestows a gift on someone. He <u>made</u> us what He freely gave us. You and I have been <u>made</u> the righteousness of God in Christ! God's life and righteousness is now our nature! That's who we are! Glory to God!! It's not the kind of gift we carry around with us. It's what we've been **Made**! So, quit trying to change who you are in Christ! Accept who you are in Him! It does not matter who you were before you got saved! It doesn't matter what you did! The person you are in Christ right now is not the person you used to be! From now on, forget about the old man and be the new man! The old man is dead! The new man is resurrected with Christ! It's time to start living a resurrected life! Get a hold of II Corinthians 5:17.

"Therefore, if anyone is in Christ, he is a new creation; old things have passed away; behold, all things have become new."

The Spirit Filled Life Bible says the word "new" in the Greek means new, unused, fresh, and novel. This word, "new" means new in regard to form or quality. Since it says all things have become new, then all the old things (he's talking about in your spirit man) have passed away. All things couldn't be new in your spirit if any of the old things are left. So, whether you feel like it or not, and despite old memories; everything in your spirit (the real you, not your mind or body) is brand new! We're not like a used car that's been cleaned up to look new. We stand now spiritually fresh and unused in the precious Blood of Jesus! We really are brand new creations in Christ! We have been made as righteous as our Father God! I thought it would be helpful in renewing our minds to look at this powerful verse in some other translations.

20th Century Translation, Revised Edition

"Therefore, if anyone is in union with Christ, he is a new being! His old life has passed away; a new life has begun!"

Amplified Bible

"Therefore if any person is [ingrafted] in Christ, (the Messiah) he is a new creation (a new creature altogether); the old [previous moral and spiritual condition] has passed away. Behold, the fresh and new has come!"

The Living Bible

"When someone becomes a Christian, he becomes a brand new person inside. He is not the same any more. A new life has begun!"

Wade Translation

"So if anyone becomes united to Christ, he is a fresh Creation; the original conditions have passed away; mark! They have been replaced by new conditions."

Phillips Translation

"For if a man is in Christ he becomes a new person altogether-the past is finished and gone, everything has become fresh and new."

Deane Translation

"...The true Christian is not merely a man altered but a man re-made..."

The Lord wants us to be so established and developed in the revelation of these Scriptures that we walk and live with a righteousness consciousness. The Apostle Paul was the greatest example of this (besides Jesus). Listen to his testimony in Acts 26:9-11.

"Indeed, I myself thought I must do many things contrary to the name of Jesus of Nazareth.

This I also did in Jerusalem, and many of the saints I shut up in prison, having received authority from the chief priests; and when they were put to death, I cast my vote against them.

And I punished them often in every synagogue and compelled them to blaspheme; and being exceedingly enraged against them, I persecuted them even to foreign cities."

It seems to me that Paul was kind of a "hit-man" for the devil. His goal in life was to destroy the Church, but we know that his life was changed forever after he met Jesus. Now listen to his testimony before the elders from the church at Ephesus. This is after he became skilled in the Word of righteousness.

"Therefore I testify to you this day that I am innocent of the blood of all men." (Acts 20:26)

Paul was guilty of the blood of a lot of men before he was born-again. You know the devil must have applied major pressure in condemnation against Paul. He was probably bringing up old memories and constantly condemning him about all the terrible things he did before he was saved. The mental

24

pressure must have seemed unbearable at times. Paul had to become skilled in the Word of righteousness just like we do. If He could overcome that kind of past, and become the kind of Believer he was, then we should never be discouraged to give up and quit, because of the bad things we've done in our past lives! How did Paul defeat this huge, negative attack against his mind? He renewed his mind to the Word of God. What part of the Word? He would have studied all the Word available, but for this area of his life, the Word of righteousness. What a gigantic blessing it must have been when the Lord gave him Romans 8:1! **"There is therefore now no condemnation to those who are in Christ Jesus..."** Wow! If you're in Christ, you have No condemnation!! Our book "The Law of the Spirit of Life in Christ Jesus" would be a great companion book to this study on righteousness.

I guarantee you that Paul meditated on that verse a lot, as well as the other righteousness Scriptures, until he quit seeing himself as he used to be, and began seeing himself as a brand new man. Again, the Apostle Paul had to grow up spiritually like we do, and put on the new man. Only faith in the Blood of Jesus could do that for Paul and us. I Thessalonians 4:7 says **"For God did not call us to uncleanness, but in holiness."** The reason we can now live a holy life is because we've been <u>made</u> God's righteousness in

25

Christ. It's not because we have strong will power. The reason we can please God in our outward lives is from the transformation of our inward lives. As I've said many times, we must learn to live from the inside out. The more we learn to live out of a righteousness consciousness, being aware of who God has made us in Christ, the more we will exhibit His holiness in our daily lives. We will live a life constantly at rest in the perfect peace of Jesus, never struggling for anything again.

CHAPTER
2

THE POWER
OF
RIGHTEOUSNESS

Many, many years ago I heard the story about what would happen if the priest went into the Holy of Holies in the Tabernacle of Moses without blood. I was totally amazed when I realized how powerful God's righteousness is. Let me remind you of this story, if by chance you have never heard it. If you are familiar with it, it will do us both good to hear it again.

The Tabernacles of Moses, according to Exodus 25-27, was a tent like structure made up of many different colored curtains. It was divided into two parts: the Holy place and the Holy of Holies (or the Holiest of All). The second section of the Tabernacle or the Holy of Holies was separated from the first section by a veil. Within the Holy of Holies was the Ark of the Covenant. The high priest went into the Holy of Holies only once a year.

"Now when these things had been thus prepared, the priests always went into the first part of the tabernacle, performing the services.
But into the second part the high priest went alone once a year, not without blood, which he offered for himself and for the people's sins committed in ignorance." (Hebrews 9:6,7)

Here is what got my attention. If the high priest went into the Holy of Holies without the blood from an animal sacrifice, he would be instantly struck dead. It wasn't because God wanted to kill him, but man, in his unrighteous nature, without a blood covering, could not live within such close proximity to God's righteous presence. After I read that, I began to realize that God's righteousness is very powerful! You may be thinking how does being cleansed by the Blood of Jesus produce power? Why do I have power because I'm righteous? Or, how is the power of God connected with righteousness? Think about this with me. Even though we are millions of miles from the sun, a stick of butter will still melt if you leave it out on a picnic table during a hot day. You could say, the stick of butter could not live or exist in the <u>presence</u> of the sun. Now the sun didn't decide it was going to try to melt the butter when you left it on the table. It was just being the sun. It was just being itself. There are things that will be destroyed if they get too close to the sun, or if they stay in its presence to long. The sun's nature is to give off light, fire and heat. That is its nature. By understanding this, we know how to protect ourselves when we go out into the hot sun; so we can act accordingly. Even when we understand what the Sun's presence can help or hurt; that doesn't change the fact that the sun is still just being the sun.

The prophet Malachi (Malachi 4:2) called Jesus the <u>Sun</u> of righteousness with healing in His wings. Just like the heat from the sun melts butter, the righteousness of God will melt and destroy sin, sickness, poverty and all the works of the devil. When the devil performs his works, it is like putting butter, so to speak, out in the presence of the sun; in this case, the Sun (Jesus) of righteousness. The devil's works will be destroyed and God's works will be performed! The book of Hebrews tells us that God is a consuming fire. The fire of God will melt away anything the devil does! Let us look back again at the

Tabernacle of Moses. According to Leviticus 16:2 & 3, the high priest could only come into the Holy of Holies (the Holy Place inside the veil) once a year with animal blood. Remember, the high priest in the Old Covenant was not born again, like believers are today. If the high priest did not come into the Holy of Holies as God instructed he would be struck dead. The high priest wouldn't be struck dead because God wanted to kill him, but because of the man's sin nature. His sin could not exist that close to God's righteousness. The high priest would die because of his connection with his sin nature. Have you ever heard a doctor tell someone, "The disease you have has spread so much in your body we cannot help you. It is true, we can kill the disease, but when we kill the disease you will die also."

Hebrews 10:1-4 says:

"For the law, having a shadow of the good things to come, and not the very image of the things, can never with these same sacrifices, which they offer continually year by year, make those who approach perfect.

For then would they not have ceased to be offered? For the worshipers, once purified, would have had no more <u>consciousness</u> of sins,

But in those sacrifices there is a reminder of sins every year.

For it is not possible that the blood of bulls and goats could take away sins."

Hebrews 9:13, 14 says:

"For if the blood of bulls and goats and the ashes of a heifer, sprinkling the unclean, sanctifies for the purifying of the flesh,

How much more shall the blood of Christ, who through the eternal Spirit offered Himself without spot to God, cleanse your <u>conscience</u> from dead works to serve the living God?"

Also read Hebrews 9:1-15. The blood of animals could cleanse man's flesh, but not his spirit. In the Old Covenant, God's people could only be ceremonially clean, or clean on the outside. Their conscience or inner man (spirit man) could not be cleansed. The blood of animals could only cleanse the <u>effect</u> of sin on the outside of man, but it couldn't remove the sin, or the sin nature in man's spirit. Because of this dilemma, the priest had to offer sacrifices continually, day after day, until Jesus could come and offer His sinless Blood for humanity once and for all. Hebrews 9:19-22 says that Moses had to take the blood of calves and goats, with water, scarlet wool, and hyssop, and sprinkle the book, all the people, the tabernacle and all the vessels of the ministry. Why did he have to do that? Because they were affected or infected by the sin in man's spirit. That revealed to us how powerful man's sin was (remember, we are still talking about how powerful righteousness is). Earlier we asked the question, "How can righteousness have power?" We could ask the same question about sin, "How can sin have power?" From these verses we see that it does have power. When sin can affect something in a negative way and cause it to be changed, then that is a demonstration of power. Look at Hebrews 9:23, 24.

"Therefore it was necessary that the copies of the things in the heavens should be purified with these, but the heavenly things themselves with better sacrifices than these.

For Christ has not entered the holy places made with hands, which are copies of the true, but into heaven itself, now to appear in the presence of God for us."

What we just read is astounding. The Tabernacle of Moses was a copy of the original Tabernacle in Heaven. The Spirit of God said the things in the earthly Tabernacle had to be cleansed from the effects of man's sin, but He also said the Heavenly things had to be cleansed. Did you really hear that? The Lord Jesus had to take His Blood into Heaven itself and cleanse the Heavenly things. We are talking about Heaven, where God lives. That showed how far Adam's sin reached; all the way to God's throne. Wow! By showing us how far Adam's sin reached, God identified how far Adam's authority or power reached! God created Adam to rule all creation. Don't tell me sin doesn't have power. The entire human race and creation were contaminated. Jesus had to suffer untold punishment and shed His priceless Blood to break the power of sin in man's life. The effect that sin (the devil through sin) has had on the human race is: spiritual and physical death, sickness, poverty and every evil ungodly thing.

Now let me show you something much more powerful than sin. Isaiah 32:17, 18 says:

The <u>work</u> of righteousness will be peace, and the <u>effect</u> of righteousness, quietness and assurance forever.

My people will dwell in a peaceful habitation, in secure dwellings, and in quiet resting places."

Being righteous in Christ isn't just a good feeling. The Bible says that righteousness works. It does something. It produces something. If I talked about the work of a home builder, I would not just be talking about a good feeling about that person's occupation, but I would be referring to the work produced from him. The work of a home builder is to build houses. He produces something. He has the power or ability to build houses. So, let me ask you this. What kind of work is produced by righteousness? **Peace**! Where does this supernatural work take place? Only in those who are righteous. This is a great work that is inclusive to Christians! Sin cannot produce this kind of work, only righteousness! We found out that Adam's sin reached all the way to Heaven. It definitely abounded, wouldn't you agree? But Romans 5:20 said that where sin abounded, grace abounded <u>much more</u>! Verse 21 in that same chapter said that grace reigns through righteousness. So, no matter how powerful sin is, righteousness is much more powerful. Sin could not stop the Blood of Jesus from making us the righteousness of God. Sin was like butter out in the hot sun, when the Sun of righteousness came into our lives! Sin didn't have a chance!

Let's go back now to Isaiah 32 again. If you are struggling to have peace in your life, then you are not allowing righteousness to do its work in you. Righteousness specializes in producing peace in our lives. The word "peace" in the Hebrew and Greek language means wholeness, something finished and completed. Another way to say that is, nothing missing and nothing broken. Therefore, the work of God's righteousness in my life is to make sure that nothing is missing and nothing is broken. If I'm sick, then healing is missing. If I'm broke, then prosperity is missing. If I'm afraid, then faith is missing. If I'm depressed, then joy is missing. If I'm broken emotionally or in any area of my life, the work of righteousness is to make me whole and complete. Praise the Lord!

Isaiah didn't say the work of Dwayne Norman will be peace. It didn't say the work of my human efforts will produce peace in my life. It didn't say getting a degree (nothing wrong with that) or having a good hobby will produce peace for me. It didn't say going to church several times a week and feeding the poor (both of these things are very important) will produce peace in my life. There are Christians who do these things and still have no peace. We can't make ourselves whole and complete, only God can. One of the main ways He does this is through developing a righteousness consciousness within us. The more we lean on our righteousness in Christ and not our flesh, the more God's righteousness will be free to work in our lives. If I hire a builder to build a home for me, but I do not allow him to do his work, then I will never live in my new house. Why don't we let righteousness do its work? The Lord suffered so much to make us righteous in Him, let's allow the power of righteousness to flow freely in our lives and to change and transform us into the very image and stature of Christ! Nothing missing and nothing broken, perfect peace!! I believe the Apostle Paul experienced this in his life. Back in chapter 1, we looked at the verse in Acts 20:26, where Paul said he was innocent of the blood of <u>all</u> men. When we remember his testimony of how he greatly persecuted the Church of God, then this verse makes Paul sound like a totally different man. Think about this. Paul put many Christians in prison to be delivered to death, but now, about eleven to twelve years after his conversion he said that he was <u>innocent</u> of the blood of all men. He was so greatly developed in a righteousness consciousness, he saw himself as a man who stood clean before the Lord. Think of the peace he walked in after knowing where he came from. That is what the work of righteousness does. That is the power of righteousness. The power of sin wanted to hold him in bondage and condemnation, but it was subject to the power of righteousness. The power of righteousness melted and dissolved that sin consciousness right out of Paul's life forever! It will do the same thing for you!!

If you are a Christian, no matter how much you have messed up your life, no matter what sins you have committed, and no matter how far you have drifted away from a close walk with the Lord, you can change all that. Come back to the Lord with all your heart and submit to His will. God can't change and restore you if you will not cooperate with Him. First, repent. Change your mind and your thinking. Spiritually, turn away from the life you have been living to a life dedicated and committed to God. Ask the Father to forgive you in Jesus' Name and He will (I John 1:9). Now, look up the "In Christ and In Him" verses in the New Testament and begin to confess and meditate on them; especially the ones that talk about your righteousness in Christ. Practice this as much as you can every day and God will develop a righteousness consciousness in you to the place where you will be able to say with all confidence and conviction, "I am the righteousness of God in Christ!" Soon, you will start experiencing the work of God's righteousness in your life. Supernatural peace from Heaven will rule your life and you will rejoice every day!

Isaiah 32:17 talked about the work of righteousness, but it also spoke of the effect of righteousness. God's righteousness can have an effect on us. In my mind that shows a demonstration of power or the ability to make a change. The effect of righteousness is quietness and assurance forever. Sin would give the opposite effect. Sin produces inner turmoil and fear (lack of assurance or lack of faith) forever. What the prophet of God said in Isaiah 32:18 would be the full effect of allowing righteousness to have its way in our lives. We would dwell in a peaceful habitation, in secure dwellings and in quiet resting places. That sounds a lot like Psalm 23.

"The Lord is my shepherd; <u>I shall not want</u>.

He <u>makes me to lie down</u> in green pastures; He <u>leads me beside the still</u> waters.

He <u>restores my soul</u>; He <u>leads me in the paths of righteousness</u> for His name's sake.

Yea, though I walk through the valley of the shadow of death,<u> I will fear no evil</u>; for You are with me; Your rod and Your staff, they comfort me.

You prepare a table before me in the presence of my enemies; You anoint my head with oil; <u>my cup runs over</u>.

Surely <u>goodness and mercy shall follow me all the days of my life</u>; and I will dwell in the house of the Lord forever."

I could have underlined the entire Psalm! Aren't you glad to be the righteousness of God in Christ? The effect of a righteousness consciousness in my life is great assurance or confidence that God is on my side. I'm one of His sons, an heir of God and a joint heir with Christ (I John 3:2; Romans 8:17)! As Jesus is at the Father's right hand in Heaven, so am I in Him on the earth (I John 4:17)! The effect of this is a confident quietness inside me. The kind of quietness within where you can lay down and take a nap in the middle of a storm like Jesus did not worried about anything! Why? Because I trust and know that my Father God has my back, especially after all He did to make me His righteousness in Christ. I know He will always cause me to triumph in every situation!!

Look with me at Hebrews 1:8,

"But to the Son He says: "Your throne, O God, is forever and ever; a <u>scepter</u> of righteousness is the <u>scepter</u> of Your kingdom.

You have loved righteousness and hated lawlessness; therefore God, Your God, has anointed You with the oil of gladness more than Your companions.""

The Lord Jesus rules His Kingdom with a scepter. A scepter is a ruling staff. It represents a king's power, authority and dominion. This verse didn't say His scepter was one of faith. He didn't call it a scepter of faith. The Father God called it a scepter of righteousness. Faith is important, without it we cannot please God. Some think all they need is strong faith to rule victoriously in life, and it doesn't matter how they live. They think it doesn't matter whether they are righteous or not, as long as their faith is strong. Remember, we were made righteous in Christ through our faith, but now we must live out that righteousness. For a king to have a scepter means he is a ruler. It implies dominion. How could he rule over his subjects if they have power over him? The king's scepter represents his power and reminds everyone that he is the ruler. The Lord Jesus rules His Kingdom in righteousness! His power and dominion are demonstrated through His righteousness! We are to rule and reign the same way over the devil, demons, disease, poverty and death! It's not about us. It's about who Jesus is, and who we are in Him! Let's look one more time at Romans 5:17.

"For if by the one man's offense death reigned through the one, much more those who receive abundance of grace and of the gift of righteousness will <u>reign in life</u> through the One, Jesus Christ."

We know the Lord reigns through righteousness because His ruling staff is a scepter of righteousness.

He told us we can reign in life also, but it will be the same way He reigns; through His righteousness and freely by His grace. It sounds like understanding the Word of righteousness is extremely important! It is strongly tied in to our living a life of victory. Could that be why many Christians are constantly experiencing defeat and depression in their lives? Is it because they are not skilled in the Word of righteousness?

In the Old Covenant, everywhere Israel went they experienced victory over their enemies; <u>as long as they had the Ark of the Covenant and obeyed God's commandments</u>. Their enemies were always defeated because of God's righteous Presence! Again, that showed power and dominion. They ruled and reigned like kings everywhere they went. No one could successfully stand against them! Their enemies represented the kingdom of darkness and sin. Every battle was a battle between God and the devil, between the power of righteousness and the power of sin. Righteousness always prevailed, unless Israel sinned or quit serving the Lord, thereby forfeiting their privileges to operate in the power of righteousness. I Samuel 5:1-4 tells of when the Philistines took the Ark of God.

"Then the Philistines took the ark of God and brought it from Ebenezer to Ashdod.

When the Philistines took the ark of God, they brought it into the house of Dagon and set it by Dagon.

And when the people of Ashdod arose early in the morning, there was Dagon, fallen on its face to the earth before the ark of the Lord. So they took Dagon and set it in its place again.

And when they arose early the next morning, there was Dagon, fallen on its face to the ground before the ark of the Lord. The head of Dagon and both the palms of its hands were broken off on the threshold; only Dagon's torso was left of it."

The Spirit Filled Life Bible said, "Dagon was the primary god of the Philistine people, with the torso, arms, and head of a man and the lower body of a fish. He was worshiped as the father of Baal." God gave the Philistines a demonstration that He was the true God and He had power over their so called "god" Dagon. At first, Dagon was fallen on its face before the Ark of the Lord, or before the righteous Presence of the Lord. That reminds me of Philippians 2:10, 11. At the Name of Jesus every knee must bow and every tongue must confess that Jesus Christ is Lord! I believe what happened to Dagon the second time is what really put fear and trembling into the hearts of the Philistines. The next time they went in there, the head of Dagon and the palms of its hands were broken off on the threshold. The power of righteousness always prevails over the power of sin or the power of the nature of sin and death!

We need to believe that everywhere we (as Believers) go the Ark of the Lord goes there also. Of course I don't mean the physical Ark. I'm talking about what the Ark represented, the righteous Presence of the Lord! When we come on the scene (at work, church, restaurants, stores, etc...) the righteous Presence of God comes on the scene! We should expect that everywhere we go the devil's works will fall down before us (before Jesus within us), and their heads and hands will be broken off before us so to speak! Expect Satan's works, his power of unrighteousness to be destroyed! We should walk and live so conscious of our righteousness in Christ that the devil's kingdom trembles with fear when they see us coming! If you read the rest of the story in I Samuel 5, you will see how the judgment of God came on the Philistines. They were struck with tumors. The Philistines recognized very quickly that the demonic power they operated in was no match for the power of God, so they put forth every effort to get rid of the Ark.

You see, the devil doesn't like us because we were created in God's image, but he especially doesn't like us when we develop a righteousness consciousness and start acting like who we are in Christ. When we do that, we become a great threat to the devil's kingdom! A Christian who has a strong righteousness consciousness will walk in a supernatural quietness and peace because he has no condemnation for sin. The devil can't get a foothold in his life. You know this must greatly frustrate the devil. He can't devour you if don't give him any place (Ephesians 4:27). This kind of consciousness in a Christian will give him great confidence and assurance to boldly and joyfully do God's will for his life! It will cause him to stand up tall on God's Word and prophesy the goodness God wherever he goes! It's even better than taking the Ark of the Lord with us where we go! We are the temple of the Holy Spirit! We are the tabernacle of God! His righteous Presence tabernacles within us!

Here is how the devil sees it in the spirit realm; everywhere you and I set our feet, the righteousness of God is displayed! The devil knows that whatever he's trying to do (through the power of sin) will be destroyed by the power of righteousness flowing through you. As you move forward in the Lord, know that the works of darkness are being annihilated and pushed out of the way, just like a big snow plow pushes the snow out of the way as it moves down the road! Now that's exciting! That makes me want to travel to different places so that God's righteousness can come on the scene! Many years ago someone asked T.L. Osborn about a country he was soon to preach in. This person made the comment that the devil was ruling that country. T.L. Osborn boldly responded, "That's because I haven't gotten there yet!" If you want an example of a righteousness consciousness, you just heard it. He wasn't speaking in pride. He was expressing great confidence in who he was in Christ! There's a big difference between the two.

Let me give you another Scripture that implies God's power is released through righteousness. Romans 6:13 says:

"And do not present your members as <u>instruments</u> of unrighteousness to sin, but present yourselves to God as being alive from the dead, and your members as <u>instruments</u> of righteousness to God."

In W. E. Vine's Dictionary of New Testament Words, he said in the Greek language, the word "instruments" could also be translated "weapons". He said the metaphor is of a military. Therefore, like a soldier uses a gun, we are to use the members of our bodies like spiritual weapons. Our members become weapons of righteousness. Before we got saved, our members were used as instruments or weapons of unrighteousness. We used our bodies to promote the agenda of the kingdom of darkness. Even though we may not have realized it at the time, we were using our members to fight (so to speak) for the devil's will to be done in our lives. That's why we pray so much for the eyes of lost people to be opened to the Truth of the Gospel. Unbelievers are so deceived by the devil. They think they are having fun living in sin and rejecting God's ways, and they don't realize they are actually helping the devil destroy their lives.

If you notice in that same verse we just read, the Lord said, **"...Do not present your members..."** The devil cannot make you use (or present) your members as weapons for sin. It is up to you to exercise your free will and present your members the way you want to use them. But also in that verse, God said something a little different to us Believers. He said before we present our members as weapons of righteousness, we must present ourselves to God as being alive from the dead. This has to do with having a righteousness consciousness. How we live on the outside is determined and affected by how we live or by what we are conscious of on the inside, in our spirits and minds. In other words, if you are not developed much in the understanding that your old nature is dead and gone, and that you have a new nature, God's righteousness, you probably won't put forth a very big effort to present your members as weapons of righteousness unto God. That is why He said to present yourself to God as alive from the dead. This is one reason why so many Christians struggle with sin in their lives. They haven't done first things first. They try their best not to sin, or they try to use their members righteously, but they haven't had any teaching on who they are in Christ. They don't have a righteousness consciousness. They want to do everything right on the outside, but everything on the inside is not correctly developed. So they are basically trying to use their will power to live the Christian life, and that is not enough. 3 John 2 says:

"Beloved, I pray that you may prosper in all things and be in health, just as your soul prospers."

This is another great verse that tells us the success of our outside life is conditioned upon the success of our inside life. So, the more developed I am in a righteousness consciousness, the more positioned I am to reign successfully in life. Can you see that there is an association or connection between being made righteous inside and reigning on the outside? There must have been a lot of power released into my life when God made me righteous, to have such a great effect on my outward life! I need to recognize this and believe it, so I can start walking in the reality of it. Ruling in every area of my life should increase in proportion to the increase of my consciousness of who I am in Christ. As I have said in many of my books, we have to learn to live from the inside out.

The reason I can be holy and live a holy life is because of what Jesus did for me in my spirit (my inner man). It is not because I have such strong will power. Will power can only go so far; especially if you have not been born again. Let me remind you of what God said in Romans 6:1,2, 6.

"What shall we say then? Shall we continue in sin that grace may abound?

Certainly not! How shall we who died to sin live any longer in it?

Knowing this, that our old man was crucified with Him, <u>that the body of sin</u> <u>might be done away with</u>, that we should no longer be slaves of sin."

Some of the Christians in Rome believed that by sinning they were bringing more glory to God. Their reasoning was, the more they sinned, the more God's grace would abound, or the more they sinned, the holier God appeared to be. We know the world is confused in their believing, but it amazes me to see how silly and unscriptural many Christians can get in their thinking and believing. Many of these believers in Rome were missing the revelation God was trying to get across to them. The revelation was their old man or old nature was dead. When they became a new man in Christ (II Corinthians 5:17, 18) everything in their spirit man was made brand new or righteous. Listen very closely. If they had understood this revelation they would not have asked such a ridiculous question. The very fact they asked this question was proof they were not convinced their old man was dead.

Let me give you an example that will clear it all up for you. Let's say that we heard on the news that a murderer named Fred was killed in the electric chair and buried the very same day. What if someone came up to you a week later and ask, "Do you think Fred is going to murder anyone else?" How would you respond to that question? That is the type of question some of the Christians were asking the Apostle Paul. Can you understand how silly it would be for someone to ask me if Fred is going to kill anyone else? That would prove he was not convinced that Fred is dead. You would not ask that question if you really believe and know that Fred is dead. Do you see how spiritually ignorant it is to ask the question, "Should we continue sinning for God's grace to abound?" That shows you are not convinced that your old man is dead; which proves you are not convinced that you are a new man made righteous in Christ.

In verse 6 of Romans 6, Paul says we need to **"know this..."** What do we need to know Paul? We need to know that since the old man is dead or was crucified with Christ; our physical bodies are no longer slaves of sin. The Spirit of God through Paul wants us to know that what Jesus did for us in our spirits, affects our natural lives. He wants us to see that because a change has taken place in our inner man, then a change can now take place in our outer man. Paul used the phrase "the body of sin" to refer to how we used our bodies in sinful ways. When he said the body of sin might be done away with, in the Greek it means rendered inoperative. That means we don't have to use our bodies to commit sin anymore. Notice I said we don't have to. We can if we want to, but we don't have to. Romans 6:14 tells us that sin does not have dominion over us, but that does not mean we cannot sin. Let me say that again. That does not mean we cannot sin. We just don't have to. The devil cannot make us sin! Even though Paul said (in verses 2 & 7) that we died to sin, that doesn't mean it is impossible for us to sin. We can sin anytime we want to, but we don't have to. When we were lost sin had dominion over us through the old nature (the law of sin and death-Romans 8:2) in our inner man. Now that the old nature is dead, our bodies can have a new master, the Holy Spirit working through our new righteous nature. With that being said, having a new nature doesn't cause our outward lives to automatically change. Romans 6:15-23 tells us we still have to present ourselves to God as alive from the dead, and our members as weapons of righteousness to God. Let me reiterate, if you are not convinced that "Fred is dead", you will not present yourself to God as being alive from the dead. That means you won't present yourself to God as a brand new creation made righteous in Christ. And if you don't do that, you will not be very successful in presenting your members as weapons of righteousness.

Let me tell you what will happen when we begin to reckon or consider ourselves to be dead to sin (Romans 6:11), and alive unto God. We will start operating as ministers of righteousness. II Corinthians 3:9 says:

"For if the ministry of condemnation had glory, the ministry of righteousness exceeds much more in glory."

Think about this with me. No one (except Jesus) in the Old Covenant was a minister of righteousness.

That was reserved for the New Covenant. To be a minister of righteousness you must be righteous. To be righteous means you have been made (on the inside) righteous. Abraham's faith was accounted to him for righteousness, as we mentioned earlier, but he still wasn't righteous in his spirit. He only had a right standing with God. That was very good, but he still was not a new creation in Christ. He could not be called a son of God, only a friend of God. You must have God's nature in you to be His son. You have to be born again to experience that depth of righteousness. This was a miracle that man could not receive until Jesus died and arose from the dead. This is the greatest miracle there is, and it was not available in the Old Covenant. No matter how close the great men and women of the Old Testament walked in "right standing" with God; He still considered their Covenant the ministry of condemnation.

In Matthew 11:11, the Lord told us that John the Baptist was the greatest in the Old Covenant, but he said the least in the New Covenant was greater than he. As great as their faith was and as awesome as God used them no one in the Old Covenant could say, "I am God's righteousness in Christ". I hope you are getting a greater revelation of what God has done for you and in you through the precious Blood of Jesus. I'm very glad to be God's friend, but a friend doesn't have the rights a son has. The most Abraham could be was a friend of God, and that was wonderful, and the Lord mightily used him. If the Lord could work so greatly through someone that was a friend of God, how much more can He do today through His sons and daughters? I praise God that I'm His friend, but your friend is not usually in your will. A friend of God is not an heir of God, or a joint heir with Jesus. A friend of God cannot say, "As Jesus is in Heaven, so am I in this world." A friend of God cannot say, "I abide in Christ and He abides in me." My name is not written in the Book of Life because I'm a friend of God. My name is written in God's Book because and only because I am His son, His righteousness in Christ! I have a right to use the Name of Jesus to do the works Jesus did and greater works because I'm a son of God! I have all power and dominion over the devil and his kingdom because I am God's righteousness in Christ! I can declare that the devil has nothing in me! I don't have his nature anymore! I have God's righteous nature in me now, but only because I am a son of God! It's great to be a friend of God, but I'm so glad it's much, much, much more than that!! Right now we are sons of God in Christ (I John 3:2)!!

II Corinthians 3:6 says that God has made us ministers of the New Covenant. He said that he made us sufficient (in Christ) as ministers of His Holy Spirit.

Since God calls the New Covenant the ministry of righteousness and we are his ministers, then we must be ministers of righteousness. That means ministers of righteousness minister the New Covenant and the Spirit of God to people everywhere we go. If we were not the righteousness of God in Christ we could not be ministers of righteousness.

In II Corinthians 11:14, 15, the Apostle Paul said:

"And no wonder! For Satan himself transforms himself into an angel of light.

Therefore it is no great thing if his ministers also transform themselves into ministers of righteousness, whose end will be according to their works."

Even the devil knows that God has made us ministers of righteousness, and he's hoping we don't find out. Look how the devil's ministers disguise themselves: as angels of light and ministers of righteousness. Our ministry is so important the devil wants to copy it. But no matter how much the devil's people try to counterfeit our ministries, it is all a façade. They can't operate in these ministries because you have to be God's righteousness in Christ. Here's the true test. Look for the fruits of righteousness in their lives. You will not find them.

In Matthew 7:15, 16, the Lord Jesus said:

"Beware of false prophets, who come to you in sheep's clothing, but inwardly they are ravenous wolves.

You will know them by their fruits. Do men gather grapes from thorn bushes or figs from thistles?"

The Lord said that inwardly they are ravenous wolves, meaning they are not righteous inwardly. Therefore, their fruit will not be a product and demonstration of the righteousness of God; even though they are portraying themselves as ministers of righteousness. Listen to what Paul prayed for the Church.

"Being filled with the fruits of righteousness which are by Jesus Christ, to the glory and praise of God."

Only those who are righteous can be filled with these fruits. Only God's sons and daughters can produce these fruits in their lives. The fruits of righteousness are a demonstration that one is walking and living in God's Divine will and purpose for his life. We talked about this earlier. The more developed we are in a righteousness consciousness the more we will be able to fulfill God's plans and purposes for our lives; the result will be fruit produced for His glory. The fruits of righteousness tie in with the fruit of the spirit spoken of in Galatians 5:22, 23. The fruit of the spirit is actually the fruit produced through our reborn spirits by the Holy Spirit. Love, joy, peace, longsuffering, kindness, goodness, faithfulness, gentleness and self-control are fruits born through a person who has been made righteous in Christ Jesus. These different fruits are evidence that God's righteousness is being fulfilled in a Believer's life. (Remember, Jesus told John the Baptist He had to fulfill all righteousness.) They are signs to the Believer that he is moving and operating in God's Divine will. They are also proof to others that he is a true minister of righteousness.

As ministers of righteousness we are called to sow the fruit of righteousness everywhere we go.

"Now the fruit of righteousness is sown in peace by those who make peace." (James 3:18)

Let me give you an example of sowing the fruit of righteousness. Isaiah 32 said the work of righteousness is peace, and peace is one of the fruit of the spirit. Again, I am not capitalizing the word "spirit" because it is not the fruit of the Holy Spirit. Yes, He is the One who enables us to produce this fruit, but this is the fruit that comes forth from a righteous man or woman of God yielding his life to the working of the Holy Spirit. When we allow the Lord to use us in ministering peace and love to a person, then we are sowing the fruit of righteousness into their lives. Let me say it this way. Salvation, healing, deliverance and miracles are God's perfect will for people. When the Lord uses you and me in ministering His saving, healing power to people, He is using us in sowing the fruit of righteousness into their lives. Proverbs 11:30 says, **"The fruit of the righteous is a tree of life..."** You could say that God is allowing the people we minister to and pray for to partake of the tree of life through us. The resurrection life of Jesus is being poured out of us for the sick and hurting. That is a true minister of righteousness. That is the kind of fruit you should expect to see. Praise the Lord!

Now, let me show you what God will do for you when you sow the fruit of righteousness into others. Let's read some familiar Scriptures in II Corinthians 9:6-11.

"But this I say: He who sows sparingly will also reap sparingly, and he who <u>sows bountifully</u> will also <u>reap bountifully</u>.

So let each one give as he purposes in his heart, not grudgingly or of necessity; for God loves a cheerful giver,

And God is able to make all grace abound toward you, that you, always having all sufficiency in all things, may have an abundance for every good work.

As it is written: "He has dispersed abroad, He has given to the poor; His righteousness endures forever."

Now may He who supplies seed to the sower, and bread for food, supply and multiply the seed you have sown and <u>increase the fruits of your righteousness,</u>

While you are enriched in everything for all liberality, which causes thanksgiving through us to God."

These are good verses for teaching on financial sowing and reaping, but that is not all. Sowing financial blessings into people lives and ministries is part of sowing the fruit of righteousness. But that is just one area. When the Lord said He will multiply the seed you have sown, He is talking about the seed of the fruit of righteousness you have sown. God said our harvest will be an increase of the fruits of righteousness in our lives, or coming back into our lives; so we will be enriched in everything for all liberality! Within that harvest coming back to us is an increase of God's perfect will being fulfilled in our lives!

Proverbs 28:1 says:

"The wicked flee when no one pursues, but the righteous are bold as a lion."

When He said the "righteous" He was of course referring to Christians, but He still did not say the Christians or the Believers are bold as a lion. He used the word "righteous" to identify which Christians He was talking about. There are Christians in this world who will even tell you that they are shy, timid and bashful. They are too afraid to witness to strangers. They are too nervous to lay hands on the sick for healing (even though Jesus commanded us to do these things in the Great Commission- Mark 16). Obviously, they are not acting bold as a lion. I believe that is where this word "righteous" comes in. I believe the Lord is telling us that the Believers who will be bold as lions and fulfill the Great Commission and do exploits in Jesus' Name will be those who have developed a strong righteousness consciousness! Those who are skilled in the Word of righteousness! Those who are bold every day to sow the fruit of righteousness! I pray that is you. If it is, look forward to a great harvest!!

CHAPTER
3

BLESSINGS
OF
THE RIGHTEOUS

I want to share with you 50 blessings of the righteous found just in the book of Proverbs. If you are a Christian, then you are the righteousness of God in Christ, and all 50 of these blessings belong to you freely from God's grace. Believe these Scriptures and expect to see all the fruits of righteousness produced in your life! Amen!

1) 3:33 God blesses their dwelling.

2)   4:18   Their path shines brighter each day like the light of dawn.

3)   10:3   The Lord will not allow them to hunger.

4)   10:6   Blessings are on their heads. They are the Blessed of the Lord and a great blessing to others!

5)   10:7   Their memory is blessed.

6)   10:11 Their mouth is a fountain of life.

7)   10:16 The labor or wages of the righteous leads to life.

8)   10:20   Their tongues are as choice silver.

9)   10:21 Their lips feed many.

10)   10:24 Their desire will be granted.

11)   10:25 They have an everlasting foundation.

12)   10:28 Their hope is gladness.

13)   10:30 They will never be removed or shaken.

14) 10:31   Their mouth flows with wisdom.

15) 10:32   The lips of the righteous know what is acceptable, they don't have a perverse tongue.

16) 11:3   Their integrity will guide them.

17) 11:4   Righteousness delivers from death. They can expect to walk in God's Divine protection.

18) 11:8   They are delivered from trouble.

19) 11:11   Their city is exalted by the blessing of the righteous.

20) 11:18   They will have a sure reward from sowing righteousness.

21) 11:21   Their descendants will be delivered. Expect God's Divine protection for your children!

22) 11:23   Their desire is only good.

23) 11:28   They will flourish like the green leaf. Expect to prosper in all you do!

24) 11:30   Their fruit is a tree of life.

25) 11:3   They will be rewarded in the earth.

26) 12:3   Their root will not be moved.

27) 12:5   Their thoughts are just or right.

28) 12:6   Their mouth will deliver them.

29) 12:7   Their house will stand. Stand on your righteousness in Christ for your whole family! Yes, they must be born again, but you have a right (righteousness in Christ) to stand in faith for their salvation (Acts 16:31)!

30) 12:10 They have regard for the life of their animals.

31) 12:12 Their root yields fruit.

32) 12:13 They will escape from trouble.

33) 12:21 No grave trouble will overtake them. No harm will befall them.

34) 12:26 They choose their friends carefully. They watch closely who they associate with. They will not let anyone lead them astray.

35) 13:5   They hate falsehood.

36) 13:9   Their light rejoices.

37) 13:21   They will be rewarded with prosperity.

38) 13:25   They have plenty to eat.

39) 14:32   They have a refuge when they die.

40) 15:6   Much wealth is in their houses. That means one of the fruits of righteousness is financial blessings!

41) 15:28   Their hearts study how to answer.

42) 15:29   God hears their prayers!

43) 18:10   The Name of the Lord is a strong tower and they run into it and are safe.

44) 20:7   They walk in integrity.

45) 21:26   They give and do not spare. They are generous givers.

46) 24:16 If they fall seven times, they will rise again.

47) 28:1 They are bold as lions!

48) 29:6 They sing and rejoice.

49) 29:7 They consider the cause of the poor.

50) 29:16 They will see the fall of the wicked.

We have an awesome inheritance in Christ! We are just as righteous as our Father God! We are the tabernacle of God's righteous Presence in the earth! We are the church on fire (see our book "Resurrection Witnesses")! I challenge you to put on Christ every day! Put on the Anointed One and His anointing, and walk tall in your position in Him as the righteousness of God!! We are the Body of Christ! His spiritual army in the land! Let's get up and go forth in Jesus' Name, and produce a lot of fruit! Glory to God!

About the Author

Dwayne Norman is a 1978 graduate of Christ For The Nations Bible Institute in Dallas, Texas. He spent 3 years witnessing to prostitutes and pimps in the red light district of Dallas, and another 3 years ministering as a team leader in the Campus Challenge ministry of Dr. Norvel Hayes. He was ordained by Pastor Buddy and Pat Harrison of Faith Christian Fellowship in Tulsa, Oklahoma in September 1980. He also taught evangelism classes several times at Dr. Hayes' Bible school in Tennessee.

Soon the Lord led him to go on the road ministering. He ministers powerfully on soul winning, and on how God wants to use all Believers in demonstrating His Kingdom not just in Word but also in Power!

He teaches with clarity, the work that God accomplished for all believers in Christ from the cross to the throne, and the importance of this revelation to the church for the fulfillment of Jesus' commission to make disciples of all nations.

He strongly believes that we are called to do the works Jesus did and greater works in His Name, not just in church but especially in the market place. As a result Dwayne experiences many healing miracles in his services, arms and legs growing out, as well as other miracles.

He and his wife Leia travel and teach Supernatural Evangelism and train Believers in who they are in Christ and how to operate in their ministries.

To inquire for meetings with Dwayne & Leia Norman, please contact them at:

Dwayne & Leia Norman
124 Evergreen Court
Mt. Sterling, KY 40353

(859) 351-6496
dwayne7@att.net
Web: www.dwaynenormanministries.org

Contact Dwayne to order his other books and products:

The Mystery DVD's (12 hours) $50.00
The Mystery (book) $12.00
The Mystery Study Guide $10.00
The Awesome Power in the
Message of the Cross $10.00
Your Beginning with God $10.00
The Law of the Spirit
of Life in Christ Jesus $10.00
Demonstrating God's Kingdom $10.00

41171043R00041

Made in the USA
Charleston, SC
22 April 2015